the days

i wait

until

i

see you

tomorrow.

poems by caitlin virginia

thank you —

dad, for teaching me how to see the world through a poet's eyes.

order—

i. bitter sleeves + tired angels.

stalled engine.

her greed.

shimmer.

daydream.

euphoria.

a day at college.

everyone cried lightning.

solid.

me.

gravity pulling the pages apart.

edge.

1989

seeing girl.

…

at dusk.

transition.

twenty.

willing to travel.

when limits seem promising.

a flourish of luxurious feeling.

ii. sunrise.

after sunset.

wish i was back in paris.

stanzas.

cat corners.

your summer.

renato.

montepaone.

greta.

vittorio

when i go.

it's a quiet 5:40 in ireland.

i sit on my bed.

shoreline.

by the end.

more stanzas.

circa 1998.

nightwind.

here, within.

iii. vulnerability in blue.

right now.

+

my superstitions yielding.

only a chair.

leaning on boys.

dylan at crossroads.

bowie.

pauper.

i am an elephant.

thanks to a friend.

i could say this to him.

the days i wait until i see you tomorrow.

i want you to see me.

preface—

there is a part of me laced with shadows.

it is not who i am anymore, but this person is very much alive.

i am from her.

the lightest prick of a needle, the softest touch of a blanket, the warmest ray of the sun. she desired these moments, but she could never find them, because it was in those moments that she was truly seen, and that was the last thing she wanted.

it is good to change, and it is good to reflect and see who we once were and how we no longer will be.

these poems are themed in romanticizing darkness and vulnerabilities, depression, curling lips and stagnant tongues.

when you feel these pieces, please know there is always someone to talk to.

you are deserving.

you are love.

you are everything.

- caitlin

bitter sleeves + tired angels.

—

it is in the days i sit and mornings i dream
where i hear the words that speak to me
in their rhythms they give me silence
it is with them that i learn how to speak

stalled engine.

"it looks like a grill"
          charred   metal bars grapple
          the iron rims
          of the car's front applique
the fumes come
          slower
          slower
finally a whisper
          breath cold like night
          we thought that's
        how far
           we'd get
you and   me   living in one place

in the dark, i just want to create
dandelion inside
blue violet surrounds

shimmer.

i started to   c r a c k

                              last night   at the   halloween
              party
              my   light began to   shine through
and i have never had to deal   with that
                                                 i have
                                                 also never had
                                                 someone care
                                                 about me that
                                                 much
                                                 most times when
                              i need to escape   i can
                              do it on my own but he just
                              wouldn't   leave me
                              he went   after
                                                       me
              when i wanted to throw myself to wolves
he cracked   me   they both cracked
me   wait, no   one
broke me   then i started to   heal   and the other
cracked   me   again it's
the never-ending cycle of emotion   everything
about   this   life   right   now   how can
i be there   for   everyone   but
still be   enough for myself? this   entire
time i have   been balancing
over a precipice   by only the tips
                                         of   my
fingers i am about to fall again
i can feel it i need   someone winter is
coming   she's gone i want   to be
free   from   myself

daydream.

whiff of grass

unfeathered bed

smokey mouth

oak barks

i turn

cobweb bites

old graves

nature path

end of season

wind speaks

i answer

shotgun-like

red steel

eyes closed

jacket

euphoria.

<pre>
            i   am   a soul
            in   a corner
            eating   my
 body
            fill it   with   arrows
            carry   me to the
 crows
            take me   away
            carry   a torch
                          to the   next
            chamber
                          how to   feel
            dead
                          it must   be
            refreshing
</pre>

a day at college.

i wake up to laughter
dry laundry
short drive
shake and fries
we dance by the still fountain
        you question everything
i taste the freedom of female
stop at the library
frequent the art section
it snows briefly
we pound our fists on the checkerboard floor
        you forget why
i take a shower before i go to sleep
smoke another cigarette
boxed wine and broccoli
turn on television
they finally leave
so i can stare at the wall
        you say my name
        i stay silent

everyone cried lightning.

the field yellows
as the sky darkens
flowers bloom
amidst the rain
tunnels of wind
spin all around you
steadily you watch
and listen
heart thumping
eyes closed
you don't feel so
lost anymore

"baby doesn't like the thunder," she cries
"or whistling!" he shouts above the fog
water trickles down his chin
"summer's heat is here," she whispers
heart low between her teeth
she shreds the red cloth at her knees
miles away a tree bursts into flames
hiding amongst its brothers
the wind erupts with tears
drops on his boots
shimmers on her cheeks
there's too much noise
make a run for it
save yourself
nature whips out a delight
crimson on her lips
on his hands
"baby didn't like us either"
run with the next
crack of thunder

solid.

a wound being salted
  skin being burned
                chew your meat
      you left on the table

     licking the rock
           arm is peeling
   after you fell
     you should be careful

            the curtain is tied
             lights dim on the crowd
          take your bow
        you laugh to yourself

me.

“quit your smoking now, you scum”
                    is what i think they think
                                        hung
                                on their thoughts
like a clothespin to cloth
ill fitting garments worn to dances
        to funerals   to bedrooms
        all pinned steaming
        unwashed desire
        unrelenting wrinkles

                            age kills us

gravity pulling the pages apart.

blue skI esna ughty r   aInbows

eu rov I s I on

                                                raw
                                    famIne
don't let the raIn fall

I   n blood and fIre

save us

please

before we ar e sanctIon ed

off

Into mold

edge.

flea bitten
rotting flesh
they're foaming
at the mouth
my instincts
yelling at me
piece of meat
that i am
dancing for them
archaic sacrifice
primal form
dripping
desperate
holding on
to the rope
holding me
down
animal

1989

poppa's in jail
momma can't call him anymore
dreamed of white-washed holy suburbans
washed down with a syrup addiction
she trusted him when he was young
innocent lies from an innocent man
didn't think he'd change his recess
to smoking pipes with women
momma let herself go
neighbors lying to her lost cat
drool staining her pillow
waking up with a dream chasing her
poppa dried up
cactus in the ocean
lying ashore after a storm
he learned how to get his feet wet

seeing girl.

look at my hands
            you see
bent knuckles
chipped blue polish
corroded nail beds
meat on sticks
look at my chest
                scarred by the past
the sun, the earth
a different world
a pumping mass
look at my face
                    back lit drowned glow
a place of safety
a place of freedom
held together by worries
an ugly truth
look at my eyes
                        wary, distant
hopeful, kind
lines of age
knowledge to see
i think
dry, feeble
                            water slits

. . .

no one here
an echo
a shadow
a passing car
sickness returns
lost in my own home
lost in my bedroom
lost in a place
that once was mine

last night we walked down to the nature reserve on south
he showed us the bamboo forest
monstrous branches reaching up to the stars
thick and heavy with creatures and things
we blew our breath to the eternal purple sky
visual emotional
soul colors different desires
i let it take control

as we escaped our woody fortress
i tripped and fell
thorns tore at my skin
leaving holes in my fingertips
i was climbing a mountain
i was tackling its peaks

we explored our inner selves
together in the bamboo forest
we portrayed our desires
to our own uncertainties
i forgot my leftovers in his fridge

transition.

in
between
side
to
side
up
and
down
flip
rotate
turn
spin
around
regret

twenty.

                i am at an adult birthday party
                there aren't any adults
                        just the guys nearby
                        whoever wants to come
                        no drama

        i am not a man
                but i verge towards it
                        am i just a shy woman
                                can i live in both worlds

willing to travel.

       i am somewhere between the earth
and the land
underground or up above
       i miss the underground
       everyone here is too bubbly and daisy
and not fucked up
our house is somewhere in between

when limits seem promising.

coming to a conclusion about who
you are   like finding a shore
amidst an endless ocean
docking the boat upon the beach
ceases any more wonder about
security   dashing to the fresh
water stream
refreshes you with clarity eating that
succulent fruit from the tree
inspiring   on the island all is new,
hopeful, limitless
hesitation becomes a catacomb in the
earth as you dig for shelter supplies
from an old wreck come in handy
for temporary survival
you ground yourself in a forlorn
promise   shaded by palm leaves

a flourish of luxurious feeling. f e e l i n g r i c h w i t h
t h o u g h t t h e o n l y e s c a p e i t s e e m s i s m y
n o t e b o o k h u m i d i t y f o n d l e s m y s k i n w r a p s m e
i n w a r m t h s t i n g s m y e y e s w i t h l i g h t n i n g s i t
a l l d a y i n b e d s i t a l l d a y i n m y h e a d d r . s e u s s
w o u l d n o t a p p r o v e h e ' d s a y g o o u t a n d f i n d
y o u r g r o o v e e v e n t h o u g h i t ' s s c a r y e v e n
t h o u g h i t w e a r s y o u t h i n e v e n t h o u g h
e v e r y t i m e y o u t a k e a s t e p b r i c k r o a d s m e l t
i n t o t h e t r e e s s e n s e s l i n g e r o n t o t h e p a s t
s t r e t c h e s m y e y e s t e a r s u p t h e p a g e s f e e l i n g
s a t i s f i e d t h e o n l y e s c a p e i t s e e m s i s m y
f u t u r e t h e d a y s w i l l c o m e i n g r e a t n o i s e s
a n d s h a p e s w o r d s o f f r e e d o m a n d c o l o r a n d
w h a t b e a u t i f u l s u n s e t s i w i l l s e e

sunrise.

—

it is in the memories and holding places
where i find myself wandering
it is in the desert where i sit and breathe
it is in the sun where i am holy living

after sunset.

you find thoughts
trailing your mind
before you sleep
those you've touched, held, loved
you wish the galaxies would connect you
with their thoughts
someone, somewhere
might be thinking about you
before they wake
then after
while eating breakfast
drinking coffee, black
smoking a cigarette, smooth
while swimming along the shore
a nap draws them in
to think of you again
then after
another meal, another smoke
down to the water again
while the colors drift by
floating with the sand
you might be their last thought
before they go to sleep
at night
after sunset

wish i was back in paris
where i find you
smoking rolled cigarettes
next to the parachute
palm trees of the eiffel
we were royals
driving near the rebellion
didn't care about money
or my regrets
underneath your sobbing
she left you on the steps
in the garden
i wiped your tears away

sallow man
slinks by unseen
he is walking
we are walking beside him

    shaggy dog
    slips by the silver stream
    he is running
    we are running after him

    silky woman
    seen by the every man
    she is sitting
    we are sitting near her

    sinking children
    startled by speaking
    they are sprinting
    we are watching them go

cat corners.

the silver light of the cafe melting into the far reaching
silence of space
filling it up with the sound that expresses through senses
when we do not use words

your summer.

feel free to walk next to me
over the grooves
antique floor boards
carrying the prince's remains
we'll divide ourselves between the face
of the clock steeped in silver
ornate with astrological symbols
where you took my picture

strangers whispering in a museum
cicadas warming their wings
dogs in dissent round backs of buildings
crawling echoes tickle humid air
the suitor hides in the rosebuds
like a cat he stalks
like a cat i trod away
vows we write down
save for later

tomorrow we will shake off the mud
from the sun beating down
where you held mine and i held yours
in the shallow wet digs of summer
my ears spring to listen
painter of words
give me your name

bright yellow beaming smile
greets me good morning
ciao, bella, he seems to say
a coat of warmth
breath for the day

montepaone.

warm houses
orange, beige, red
warm people
tan, worn, humble
warm air

greta.

she'll swing right by you
if you don't look ahead
she'll dance to the doors
you'll wish you were dead
she'll make you cry
where were you in your head
she'll roll with the consequences
loose under shorts red

beyond the arc of his brow
are piles of earth for eyes
i see him there
around his globe spills
a horse's mane
his body draped in strides
nothing to hide
walking skeleton bent like wire
sinister grin
with a heart full of sweet wine
he lives in a dim corner
hands work as good as forty years do
feeds the neighboring cats
a forgiven priest
a humble artist
he found himself in davoli

when i go.

where horizon floats on the sea
where cerulean sky lets it be
where iridescent hours stay true
where royal landscape is new
where blueprint of time slows
where lesser of burdens go
where warmth of the earth glows
where we find copanello

it's a quiet 5:40 in ireland.

it's a quiet 5:40 in ireland
only a few muffled daydreams escape
the whispering lands of the dark
drenched in perspiration
they run like a wildfire ebbing away in a forest
mortal enemies lay standing in the smoke shadow
heartbeats hold hands
watch how time unfolds once again
brings us all together in a wasteland of deception
can you feel the rain
i ask the girl in bunk 8
the leaves
the sap
the skeletons
it's in the ground
she answers me
pouring snores of thought rumble out
the last crisp flame throws itself into the light
i fall asleep

i sit on my bed.

i sit on my bed with my laptop
i tried to patch up my ceiling with duct tape
the rain was coming through
it didn't work
now instead of one solid drop
there are four small drops
where there was a leak
now there is four
until the rain stops there will be a hole in my ceiling
when there is no rain i do not notice it

shoreline.

me in my clothes
you in your beads
what an odd pair of twins we make

by the end.

loving isn't always blind
sometimes when you close your eyes
you forget how to see

waking up is refreshing
ice on the back of your neck
finishing a long run
discovering a secret hideaway
where only you can be

beyond lost fingers, cells of fuel
wrought-iron wastes and battle scars
a right of passage stands more cruel
than our rioters' devout seminars

can i meet you in the stars
while you're reeling on yesterday
sure fire scotch, a pint of soul
to find ourselves is the only way

circa 1998.

mother and daughter
coloring on the deck
filling in the shapes
mother holds shell
to her ear
gasps
daughter looks alight
sitting in her highchair
wonder
she holds out her small palm
the width of the baby conch
fits perfectly
she holds it to her ear
to mimic and to listen

nightwind.

indigo
violet
fuschia
orange
lavender
sky blue
pale white moon
all shades of blue
fly by the curtain of the clouds
curtains of the land
edges and rounded peaks
glides through them
soundless to the atmosphere
familiar to the earth
and travelers' continental gifts
night wind guide
hum inside
we soar

here, within.

summer's heat reminds me of
nights i feel alone
yet i feel strange comfort
by the atmosphere
i now understand
how space understands me

vulnerability in blue.

—

it is in the nights i wander and find the visions
waiting the stars watching me
it is in the chance of seeing you in a dream
that i long for the sun to end

right now.

i don't have words
everything has changed
and for that
i am changed
and for that
nothing will be the same
it doesn't feel real
as much as i know that it is
as much as i know that i am
and where he is
lost in this country
and now
here we are
in slow motion
carving steel

+

<table>
<tr><td>

this is her:
valleys
oceans
murmurs
mud
crickets

</td><td>

this is him:
humming
mirrors
nests
grass
caves

</td></tr>
</table>

my superstitions yielding.

you know the look
         the look
         the look

when you miss the moment you can hear the slightest breath like a
         whimper wishing there were more times like this you could
         spend time brushing each other's' arms

                         spilling onto the floor
                         rubbing through bone
                         seeping through ceiling

you know the look
         the look
         the look

when you're on the opposite side of the room as soon as you finish
         scanning the faces of strangers you lock eyes almost like
         no one else's eyes would ever matter they're already looking
         at you

                         when you see everything
                         that one brief second
                         does anyone notice

you know the look
         the look
         the look

when time has passed and nothing happens the briefest of grimaces
         of skepticism of restraint flashing it's as if all the events
         that took place before then leading to now leading to
         letting go

what we wanted
what we have
always speaking

you know the look
        the look
        the look

when every time we can only remember our arms wrists fingers
        dancing to the sounds of the hum of the car when we got
        too close when our eyes couldn't look away

                who we're seeing
                where we're breathing
                between you and i

only a chair.

restless mind   collapsed

on my heart   my shoulder

light rain   light tears

helpless

a chair

resting   he returns

    darker

        bitter   with   himself

    bends   over,   in   short

        no   words

    i'm   not one   to say no

leaning on boys.

small, meaningless
a branch on a tree
a foot taller
than my head
a year younger
kept to himself
besides our conversations
in the hallways
he waited
resting on a locker
my heart unrest
twenty-four hours
until the minute
i said no
and it crumbled
sank, fell away
a friendship
gone
because
he thought
i was pretty
sour eyes
now distilled
he went after his wants
but i didn't

dylan at crossroads.

boy walking down a sidewalk track
nothing but a cape on his back
the sky is falling all around him
he can't even lift his chin
that is very nice
there is nothing you can do
king of comics

bowie.

i could feel a hum in the air
as we walked up west barnard
the light rain misted over the noise
loosening the tight grip around our throats

somewhere in my mind
was a grin awaiting its fortune
a heartbeat bubbling to the surface
as we walked up west barnard

he scratched out the truth
a couple times before admitting it
he spilled a confession down my shirt
it was the shape of paisley

pauper.

there's poking prodding
        green eyes soaking
        into my back
                    i take a walk across
                    the dewy field
                    sweet smiles
                    long hugs
        he fills my arms
a blonde   affection
        grasping my face
        gasping
        crying
        admittedly
        over some   boy

i am an elephant
magnificent
today i feel
powerful

i have big choices
permeating
i am humble
patient

i wander the dunes
confident
no one can see
ignorant

i am led to water
temptation
safe to return
stumbling

i am an elephant
commanding
look me in the eye
forgive me

thanks to a friend.

brick-shoulders
he was a friend of mine
he held me up tirelessly
like a child letting me sit there
walking on a sunset path
feeling like a storm

he gave me a gift, once
subtle in his sense of humor
a pair of pants he made
laughing, i cried
i gave him all of my thoughts
in a journal made of paper

he left me on a table
he awakened a thought
dormant in my chest
he peeled open my inky ribs
stuffed some air in there
and i was breathing

he is distant like the sea
wide, vast, moving
 in distress
pulling in
 different directions
dragging down
 to their depths
  a man a woman
unaware of his impact
the suffering

    please

     drown

the days i wait until i see you tomorrow.

what do you do

when you start to feel

do you risk it all
and tell the one
you want to tell everything

or do you let it burn
each day growing
finally have to burst
you don't know how you'll burst
or who you might hurt when you explode

i told him

for the first time in my life

no playing games   no lies no secrets just honesty
now the future is uncertain
once a friendship
now a mystery
will he reciprocate
will i let these feelings pass
people can surprise you in the most
unexpected ways...
feelings came at the wrong time
they came right
as he started to develop feelings
for her
right when he needed me
just like she needed him
but he looks at her like a
monster

right when i felt there was

no one
who
 cared
about
 me

wrong
now that i'm left stuck in
this helpless little hole
why did i tell him?

because if i didn't
it would eventually consume me
everyday would be worse than the last
because if i didn't
i would never know
because if i didn't
i'm never honest
it is compulsive

i told him
i'm so proud of myself for that
while i'm a little embarrassed
he's going to look at me in a whole different light
could be what i needed

i told him

because i know how much he cares about me
he knows how much i care about him
why was he surprised
i don't know
i was surprised he was surprised
why didn't he
feel the same way?
right now
there's hope
light at the end of   a tunnel   i may
never
reach

raw eyes
behind a smile
tongue tied
big romantic
heart like a lover
spill staining the world
don't worry
about the mess
they say you are kind
you are in your head
be friendly
you are
a painting

Caitlin Virginia (she/they) is an independent artist. This is their first self-published book of poetry following the release of their self-produced EP *Insider*.

@caitlinviirginia | caitlinvirginia.com